Watch the Company You Tweet:

4 Step Guide to Making an Impact on Twitter

By: Joy Cook

Watch The Company You Tweet: 4 Step Guide To Making An Impact On Twitter

For information contact; PO BOX 36241, Greensboro, NC 27416

www.JoycookPR.com

Book Cover design by: By Way of Design, Anthony Burno
ISBN-10: 1505452783
ISBN-13: 978-1505452785
First Edition: January 2015

10 9 8 7 6 5 4 3 2 1

Dedication

To Mrs. Mary Lee Edwards, my maternal Grandmother and the matriarch of our Family:

Your wisdom and guidance are priceless and we are so blessed that the fruit doesn't fall too far from the tree. Even though you aren't able to read this book with your eyes, I know you will listen and read it with your heart.

Your Loving Granddaughter,

Joy

Foreword

Watch the Company You Tweet: 4 Step Guide to Making An Impact on Twitter is more than a how-to- book, it's Joy Cook's journey from her early days of Twitter to becoming a 'twitter guru'. It's a journey of commitment and innovation in a profession she loves – Public Relations.

My association and journey with Joy started in 2002 when she was a student in my public relations class at our university. Those were the days when interactive technology was just surfacing and Twitter was not even on the radar. PR practitioners depended mainly on traditional methods of pitching to media through email, phone, and faxes and, occasionally, the web. Joy embraced and excelled in her courses utilizing the traditional media of the day and soon realized her passion and professional calling. She discovered her powerful draw to serving as a voice of advocacy for organizations seeking opportunities, confronting challenges, and facing crises.

In the ensuing years, as my relationship with Joy transitioned from teacher to public relations colleague, Joy took the fundamentals of PR to a new level. Then, as today, I'm in awe of Joy and her success. With her insatiable curiosity and intuitive sense of the power of technology as a mode of dialogue and collaboration, Joy has been able to leverage technology to develop meaningful relationships. In 2007 Twitter was still in its infancy stage; however, Joy had the vision to appreciate the potential of it to reach and engage key publics in a new and powerful way. She became an early adopter of Twitter (in spite of its strange name). With just one click, Joy was able to connect to multiple audiences and develop connections in minutes rather than weeks or months. Joy soon became a star in the world of Twitter, a journey that took her to the White House and to the 2012 Democratic Nation

Convention.

Today, Joy tirelessly works to share her skills and talents in her webinars, teleconferences and personal appearances. Her deep knowledge of the world of technology and Twitter has helped others in their quest for a meaningful professional life in public relations and public life. Now, with the publication of her book, *Watch the Company You Tweet: 4 Step Guide to Making An Impact on Twitter,* Joy shares her knowledge with you in an engaging, conversational manner. Each page provides easy to understand, comprehensive, step by step, no-nonsense "how-to" ways to help you market and leverage your own success. With more than 85% of customers expecting businesses to be active in social media but so few doing it effectively, I encourage you as an individual or as a business person, to become a proactive leader - join the twitter conversation, network, and get your message out and have your voice heard. Enjoy the Twitter journey – it's exciting and rewarding! *Patricia Fairfield-Artman, Ph.D.*

Table of Contents

Introduction:

Don't Give a twit about Twitter? … It's time you reconsider.

On August 30, 2008, I sent my first tweet, "Expanding my territory." At the time I did not know just how much that statement would ring true. Since 2008, I have been using Twitter to communicate with millions of people all over the world. Who would've thought that with just 140 characters (not words, but characters), movements would be sparked and the world would change? I remember being the first and only person in my immediate circle on Twitter, which forced me to interact with people I did not know. Some of those people were Maria Shriver, Brittney Spears, Tyrese Gibson, and even the leader of the free world, President Barack Obama (Yes, They all follow me on Twitter- any many more influencers.) Now you may think, wait a minute, these people probably have other people tweeting for them. Now they may, but back in 2008 it was real...Twitter was being operated by the Influencers themselves. As a matter of fact that is what Twitter is all about...who is influencing the Influencers. In 2009, I took my first and only Twitter workshop led by a brilliant trailblazer in Health Care Tweetchats recognized by the Mayo Clinic. Her final words to the group were: "Don't Give a twit about Twitter?....It's time you reconsider." This is when Twitter went from being a toy to me to a tool that got me to the White House in 2012 and into some of the most trusted circles of Influencers in the world. In this book, I take you through a proven four step process to change your Twitter account from a toy to a tool that will make an IMPACT. *Watch the Company You Tweet: 4 Step Guide to Making An Impact on Twitter* is written to show you not only how to use Twitter but how to use Twitter right.

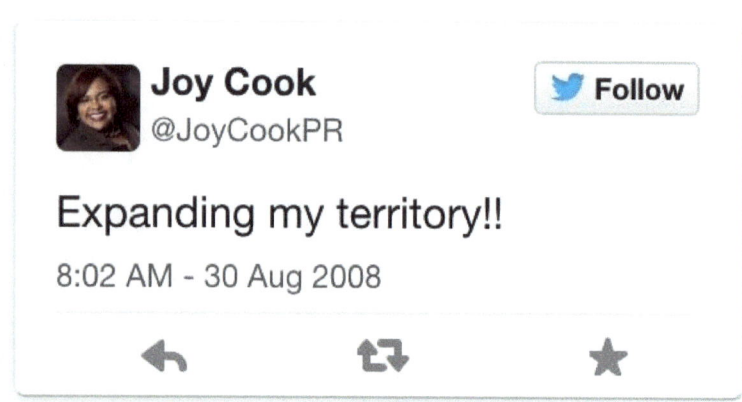

Chapter 1

ENGAGE (Step 1)

en·gage

inˈgāj,enˈgāj/

verb

1.

occupy, attract, or involve (someone's interest or attention).

Social Media is a great equalizer. There is a shift happening all over the world! I like to call this shift the social media revolution. We have access to more information than ever before in history. Social Media is a great contributor to this paradigm shift. With access to more information comes the ability to get your cause, product, or business to millions of people in a short amount of time. Did you know, 73% of online adults use social networking sites? Just think about how just 10 years ago this was a foreign way of life. Research shows that if your business is not on social media today, in five years you won't exist. Twitter is the most misunderstood social media site. Twitter has real business value and most people don't even know it.

Twitter is my "sweet spot". Twitter's foundation uses a principle that is my favorite thing to study: Social Capital. Social Capital is in its basic definition, popularity.

Social Capital is superseding in some cases regular capital. Here is where the "magic" happens. To be a standout success in the sea of information you must *engage* your audience. Content is king and creating a strategy for your online communication will make the difference. You have to tell your company's stories in a way that makes you stand out from the crowd and that organically grows your online community. Let's face it: the average American's attention span in 2013 was about 8 seconds. The average attention span in 2000 was 12 seconds. And then get this kicker - the average attention of a goldfish is 9 seconds. So in order to make an impact you must grab the reader's attention almost immediately. In this chapter I will show you exactly what you need to do today to standout.

Why is Twitter so important? Twitter is so important because it makes use of only 140 characters and is the new way to syndicate your message into the feeds of influential people easily and for FREE! The First word in the definition of engage is: occupy. Your tweets must occupy a space long after you hit send to begin to make an impact. For example, my first tweet of every day since I have been on Twitter is, "Thank God for a new day!!!". The way that specific tweet lasts long after I send it is through retweets and favorites by other people who follow me on Twitter. Wait a minute Joy, you say. "What is a retweet? What is a favorite...a follower...heck...What is Twitter?" I am passionate about Twitter, can you tell? I will slow down and map out the fundamentals.

Twitter is a social media site that allows its users to communicate to each other in 140 characters or less. According to Wikipedia, "Twitter is an online social networking service that enables users to send and read short 140-character messages called "tweets". Registered users can read and post tweets, but unregistered users can only read them."

Engagement as defined by the campaign's purpose and objective is denoted by an increase in the awareness of and support by key stakeholders as well as to proactively manage statements and accusations. My public relations and digital engagement firm does exactly that. We provide greater awareness for fans and followers and grow online communities via the strategic use of various social media platforms. Twitter was especially targeted in most of our Crisis campaigns because of its ability to provide real-world, real-time impact and engagement of the media, fans, and constituents.

Part of the advice I give is to do a Twitter competitive analysis: Take a look at how your "competitors" or other prominent people in comparable businesses to see how they are facilitating conversations on Twitter. In many cases you should see what they are doing as a guide not to copy their exact method. Engaging your audience on Twitter is not a one size fits all deal.

In this chapter and the following, I have provided exercises for you to start designing the perfect twitter strategy:

Tweet Engagement Assessment

Three mentors I follow on Twitter are
1.
2.
3.

Three great things about my brand are
1.

2.

3

Three great things about my products, services, and/or offerings

1.

2.

3.

Three great verbs that describe my mission and vision are

1.

2.

3.

Chapter 2

EMPOWER (Step 2)

em·pow·er

əmˈpou(ə)r/

verb

give (someone) the authority or power to do something.

Because of Twitter's real-time engagement with users, it is my preferred method and primary focus used to empower brands and to execute the social media strategies that I create. Within the first 60 seconds of a tweet being sent I have reached approximately, 78,000 people. Wow! You can't do that on Facebook, Instagram, Pinterest, or any other platform.

As a result of our strategic and comprehensive efforts in an online Crisis Management campaign that I facilitated over a short period of time, my company **reached approximately 2.6 million Twitter accounts!**

This was achieved by retweets and mentions relevant to the specific content of this tweet, which increases twitter impressions and penetration of constituents and key stakeholders. Many movements have been sparked by empowering people on Twitter. This is how the Arab Spring happened.

The Arab Spring: is a revolutionary wave of demonstrations and protests (both non-violent and violent), riots, and civil wars in the Arab world that began on December 18, 2010 and spread throughout the countries of the Arab League and surroundings.

If you empower enough people you can spark a movement and change a country or even the world. Research shows that a retweeted message will reach, on average, 1000 people, no matter how many followers you have. Retweets are just as important, if not more, than simply the number of followers. (The average tweet is retweeted 1.4 times).

.

Empowering people through Twitter allows for: Coordination, Communication and Collaboration. Twitter is swiftly becoming the #1 evangelism tool.

Take a Twitter Timeout

Take a moment to answer these questions to empower your followers:

Questions:

- Consciously think about: How do I frame my tweets?
- What is my cause or business history?
- Can the world truly be changed in 140 characters or less?
- What is the importance of my relationships on and off-line?
- Who are my influencers? How does social capital play a role in what I do?

- What are some memorable messages transported through Twitter?

Tweet Empowerment Assessment

Three causes I follow on Twitter are
1.
2.
3.

Three causes I promote on Twitter are
1.
2.
3.

Three of the most powerful value propositions I bring to Twitter
1.
2.
3.

Three great verbs that describe things I am passionate about
1.
2.
3.

Chapter 3

EXCITE (Step 3)

ex·cite

ikّsīt/

verb

1.

cause strong feelings of enthusiasm and eagerness in (someone).

If you can get enough people excited about what you are talking about, you have a greater chance at converting them to customers and supporters. Our identity is usually attached to somebody or something else. In this chapter, why and how is what I will show you. Be intentional with your message. Again, remember that you only get 140 characters. You can tell more about a person in 60 seconds on Twitter than you can by reading a one page bio, if you excite them. Think about it, a newspaper heading, "Extra, Extra, Read All about It !"... (along with a catchy topic/MESSAGE to the reader) is about 140 characters. Therefore, you will want to make every tweet have the same impact as a newspaper heading.

A 30 second commercial is a traditional public relations tactic that is used to help win interviews and gain influence. The thought process behind this is that a person should know your strengths and why they should hire you within the first 30 seconds of you speaking. It's the same mindset with Twitter; but, instead of getting 30 seconds, we now only get 8 seconds because of short attention spans and instead of speaking your words, you are typing them. The new 30 second commercial on Twitter will excite your online community!

Your Twitter bio should be exciting as well! Check out this example:

@bizarroguy
The man your #librarian warned you about. Former audio engineer, now #author, #editor, future #corpse.

To give you more specific tips on crafting an exciting Twitter bio I will share excerpts from -: http://www.howdesign.com/how-design-blog/4-steps-to-a-better-twitter-bio/#sthash.FAEaiUoy.dpuf

As the mere existence of a website entitled, Twitter Bio Generator, suggests, crafting a memorable bio involves some forethought. An extension of your personal brand, this bio should tell others who you are in an informative, entertaining way that encourages all who stumble upon your account to click "follow." And, like most quality writing, it needs to be concise – 160 characters to be exact.

If your existing bio only reads, "graphic designer," "social media guru," or worse sits empty, check out these steps from Robin Landa's latest book, Build Your Own Brand, to craft a Twitter bio that's interesting, informative, and let's face it, probably a little ironic.

1. Start with an extreme point of view

This extreme statement should hook your readers' interest, so the more outrageous the better. Odd combinations or juxtapositions work well.

Ex: Lee Clow's (**@leeclowsbeard**): "Musings on advertising and facial topiary. Usually daily. Often dandruff-free."

2. Write a straightforward bio statement

This straightforward statement is the informative part of your bio. Use it as an opportunity to tell readers about your work, hobbies, interests, etc.

You may also consider using this part of your bio to reference current projects and/or companies you work for. This lends credibility to your Twitter handle and suggests what readers can expect to find in your tweets.

It's also worthwhile to include links to your blog, website, and other social media sites. To keep your bio at the 160-character limit you can include one website in your bio and another in the designated website section.

Jessica Walsh's bio (**@jessicawalsh**) provides a good example. She links to her studio's Twitter page (**@sagmeisterwalsh**) within her bio, and also includes the studio's website in the aforementioned section.

3. Find a way to relate the two

This step can present a challenge. Try thinking of ways to relate the extreme hook and straightforward statement that would surprise and entertain readers. Write several different versions.

Ex: Margrethe Lauber (**@profLauber**): "I teach art history and graphic design to impressionable (and sometimes brilliant and talented) young minds at a small ag/tech college in rural NYS."

4. Refine your statement

And I would add EXCITE your audience.

Tweet Excitement Assessment

Three reasons I retweet people on Twitter are
1.
2.
3.

Three reasons I am retweeted on Twitter are
1.
2.
3.

Three of the most exciting Twitter accounts I follow are
1.
2.
3.

Three ways I excite and ignite a movement in 140 characters
1.
2.

3.

Chapter 4

EXCHANGE (Step 4)

ex·change

iks'CHānj/

noun

1.

an act of giving one thing and receiving another (especially of the same type or value) in return.

Twitter is conversational. For someone like me who is a self-proclaimed conversationalist it was intuitive and natural for me to fall in love with Twitter. I have degrees in Communication Studies (Sociology), and English so little did I know my studies had been preparing me for the exchanges I would have on Twitter later in life. Being intentional about who, what, when, where and how you have these exchanges on Twitter is the difference maker. For example, Twitter is about influence and if you want your message to travel far, you need to get the attention of Influencers that follow you and have them RT your tweet.

If I have 5,000 followers on Twitter and 2 people who also have 5,000 followers RT me, I have reached 15,000 people in mere seconds. It is also true that if I have one follower who has 15,000 followers I reach the same number of accounts. However, if the 15,000 accounts are not people or businesses with influence the same level of impact doesn't happen. This is where strategy is important. The intention is to foster meaningful interactions with key influencers because these people serve as subtle ambassadors to program the messages proactively and to syndicate messages. *Strategies last forever and Tactics are temporary.*

Strategic efforts on Twitter are intended to build online community awareness, as well as to increase conversations and beneficial relationships with people who may be unfamiliar with who you are and what your cause is.

In the definition of exchange, "an act of giving one thing and receiving another in return" (especially of the same type or value). In return is exactly what you want to happen in the Minute by Minute exchange on Twitter.

What is a hashtag? The hash or pound sign (#) is used on Twitter along with a a word or phrase preceded by a hash or pound sign (#) and used to identify messages on a specific topic.

Why I am a #hashtag evangelist: Hashtags are a way of categorizing information on Twitter as well as a way to see what's popular and who is tweeting about a certain subject.

Little known Twitter tip: Register your hashtag at www.twubs.com to claim administrative rights over the hashtag(s) you use the most.

It is important when carving out your space in the Twittersphere that you brand each tweet with your name and/or cause. For example: #Joy Cook PR

Tweet Exchange Assessment

Three of the most powerful exchanges I've had on Twitter
1.
2.
3.

Three of my most memorable exchanges on Twitter
1.
2.
3.

Three of my goal exchanges on Twitter (For example: My goal is for the President of the United States to RT me)
1.
2.
3.

Three exchanges I plan to make in the next 30 days
1.
2.
3.

Chapter 5

Men Lie, Women Lie, but numbers don't -Analytics and ROI

Now that you have gone through the 4 Step process: ENGAGE, EMPOWER, EXCITE, and EXCHANGE. You are now ready for the empirical proof. Twitter is the only medium you can reach millions of people in 30 seconds for FREE. The only investment is your time. The way you know what you are doing is working is the same as with any other business or scientific method...the numbers.

There are several analytic systems I use to test strategies and show ROI. My favorite is Tweetreach.com, a system that gives you a free snapshot of how far your tweet traveled. Consequently, to get a complete report, there is now a small charge. This report certainly proves to be more than worth the investment.

a.   Tweetreach report (www.tweetreach.com)
b.   Klout (www.klout.com)
c.   Peerindex (www.peerindex.com)

Klout is a website and mobile app that uses social media analytics to rank its users according to online social influence via the "Klout Score", which is a numerical value between 1 and 100.

Klout scores measure user influence within social media, with influence being defined as the ability to move others to action. The average active twitter user has a Klout score of *20*, and typically sees an increase in Klout score in 2-4 four weeks based on a variety of factors.

My Klout score on my personal Twitter account is *70*. Do you see

now, why I am influencing the influencers?

Peerindex: is a London-based company providing social media analytics based on footprints from use of major social media services.

Bonus Chapter

90 days until Rock star status

In my Public Relations firm, I give one-on-one digital engagement and public relations strategy sessions. This sample report, worth ($250 USD), is my gift to you. Follow the steps in this report to take your business and your brand from oblivion to making an impact in 90 days:

Summary

These recommendations result from a one-on-one strategy session. The seven points outlined, reinforce the importance of improving your online presence and implementing them accordingly will ensure the success of future digital engagement on Twitter.

To be done within 30 days

Twitter -Make connections: Follow all relevant mentors and anyone they follow. Connect with and follow integral people in your field. (at least 10)

1. Create a "Twitterfeed" www.twitterfeed.com with favorite blog.
2. #creativechangeagentRegister your #hashtag at www.twubs.com
3. Create a custom 30 second commercial.
a. Update LinkedIn profile with your 30 second commercial
b. Create a dropbox file with ALL conventional media appearances

c.   Send a press release to launch all completed social media and announcing the launch of your speaking and media appearance availability.

d.   List all of your "credible points" that make you an expert on pertinent topics.

To be done within 60 days

4.   Build your email list – create a word document or excel spread sheet for easy access to addresses.

a.   Website – www.watchthecompanyyoutweet.com

b.   email sign up option

c.   Who, what, when, where, how –

d.   Outline entire website on paper

e.   Create names for possible website pages

5.   Networking

a.   Attend at least one event that you publicize on Twitter and cross promote on the different Social Media.

b.   Document any key and/or notable attendees.

* Send Twitter Thank yous to new followers and re-tweeters

* Use Hootsuite to plan when and how often you will tweet

* Implement strategies in 30 day increments

* Tweet no less than 3 times a day during the first 30 days

Frequently Used Twitter functions:

DM- Direct Message

RT- Re-Tweet

#ThrowbackThursday

#FF- Follow Friday

#FlashbackFriday

Trending- Most popular #hashtags on twitter

Chapter 6:

Ms. Twitter: Joy Cook Goes to Washington: #WHTweetUp Experience

According to the White House website (www.whitehouse.gov), a few times a year, they open the doors to the White House and host special "White House Social" events for people who engage with us on social media. Back in 2012, I was one of the inaugural White House Tweetup participants for the arrival ceremony of the Prime Minister of Great Britain and Ireland. This is a new phenomenon started with this administration. The transparency facilitated by the Obama administration is unprecedented. The President of the United States invited influential Tweeters from all over the country to engage a Tweetup during the arrival ceremony. We also had the opportunity to meet with members of the President's administration including then Press Secretary, Jay Carney.

I got the attention of the White House on Twitter, then I filled out a short application and as a result, I was selected to become a part of history! No other way or medium would have gotten me here ...to this moment.

When I got to the White House I was in awe! The feeling was surreal to be beside Presidents, Prime Ministers and other dignitaries, ... all because of Twitter!

When I introduced myself to The President's then, Deputy Chief of Staff and Director of Public engagement, Jon Carson, he said, "Joy Cook, hey I know you! ... I follow you on Twitter." At that moment I knew there was no turning back for me and I was one of the Influencers ...influencing the Influencers.

Congratulations! You've been selected to attend
the WhiteHouse Tweetup.
Please join us for the
Official Visit of Prime Minister David Cameron of the United
Kingdom of Great Britain and Northern Ireland and his wife,
Samantha Cameron
Wednesday, March 14th, 2012
The White House
IMPORTANT: Because people may be traveling to attend the
event in Washington, D.C., we want to set clear expectations.
This invitation is to attend an arrival ceremony on the South Lawn
of the White House on the morning of March, 14th and an
opportunity to engage with Administration officials after the
ceremony. You will be outdoors for the arrival ceremony portion
of the tweetup. You will receive further details on arrival
information upon receipt of security information and RSVP.

The President and Mrs. Obama

invite you to attend the

ARRIVAL CEREMONY

honoring

The Right Honorable

David Cameron, M.P.

Prime Minister of the United Kingdom

of Great Britain and Northern Ireland

and Mrs. Samantha Cameron

to be held at

The White House

on Wednesday, March 14, 2012

at 9:00 a.m.

Gate opens at 7:00 a.m. and closes promptly at 8:30 a.m.
Please enter at the Southeast gate,
15th Street and E Street, NW.

The ceremony will be held outside on the South Lawn.
In case of inclement weather, this event will be cancelled.
Please call (202) 456-7041 for further information
after 6:00 p.m. on March 13, 2012.

Official Invitation from the 44th President of The United States of America, Barack H. Obama

Pictured: Joy Cook in front of the White House participating in the Arrival Ceremony of the Prime Minister of Great Britain

Pictured: Joy on the front page of the Greensboro News and Record

The Role Twitter Played in the 2012 Democratic National Convention

Twitter is the new grassroots –Joy Cook

No matter what side of the aisle you sit on, there were many bi-partisan lessons learned from the historical role Twitter played at the 2012 Democratic National Convention (DNC). FACT: those who do Twitter well win elections. History was made on September 7, 2012. Night three of the Democratic National Convention President Obama's speech set a record.

From September 7, 2012 Notes:

Today's highly-anticipated event in Charlotte was the single biggest day of both conventions. President Barack Obama's (@BarackObama) acceptance speech at #DNC2012 set a new record for political moments on Twitter, with **52,756** Tweets per minute coming just after its conclusion.

The Democratic National Convention has driven an incredible amount of Twitter conversation since the very first day— through the close of the official proceedings, we have seen more than 9.5 million Tweets sent about the events in Charlotte. Just the final day of the convention delivered roughly 4 million Tweets— approximately equal to the total number from the entire Republican National Convention.

Many of today's 4 million Tweets were sent during the President's acceptance speech. @barackobama delivered a great collection of tweetable lines this evening, and Twitter responded accordingly. His five top peaks in Tweets per minute were actually all higher than any other moment for a speaker in either convention. The moments in his speech that elicited the biggest Twitter reactions were:

- 43,646: "I'm no longer just the candidate, I'm the President"
- 39,002: "I will never turn medicare into a voucher"
- 38,597: Discussing Medicare
- 37,694: "We don't think government can solve all our problems..."
-34,572: Quips about the Olympics and "Cold War mind warp"

Vice President Biden's (@JoeBiden) speech also inspired a fair share of Tweets, peaking at 17,932 TPM. Another notable moment was former Rep. Gabrielle Giffords' (@GabbyGiffords) moving delivery of the Pledge of Allegiance, with 3,278 TPM— higher than any of the next three speakers who followed her.

In addition to the commentary from political pundits, the stars were out on Twitter tonight sharing their own views of the President's performance:

My personal historical journey with Twitter during the Democratic National Convention:

@JoyCookPR defined as Influential

rosenquista Annmarie Rosenquist
Julian #Castro was the first Latino to keynote a #DNC convention but his adorable daughter has stolen the spotlight http://t.co/7KjhRXAR ^kr
09/05/2012　Reply　Retweet　Favorite

flowersliz Liz Flowers
Julian #Castro was the first Latino to keynote a #DNC convention but his adorable daughter has stolen the spotlight http://t.co/7KjhRXAR ^kr
09/05/2012　Reply　Retweet　Favorite

yourvoices Nikita Shearin
Julian #Castro was the first Latino to keynote a #DNC convention but his adorable daughter has stolen the spotlight http://t.co/7KjhRXAR ^kr
09/05/2012　Reply　Retweet　Favorite

joycookpr Joy Cook Influential
Julian #Castro was the first Latino to keynote a #DNC convention but his adorable daughter has stolen the spotlight http://t.co/7KjhRXAR ^kr
09/05/2012　Reply　Retweet　Favorite

prnpolicy PR Newswire Policy
Julian #Castro was the first Latino to keynote a #DNC convention but his adorable daughter has stolen the spotlight http://t.co/7KjhRXAR ^kr
09/05/2012　Reply　Retweet　Favorite

jazzmast3r Abram Soto
San Antonio Mayor @JulianCastro's daughter steals the spotlight. WATCH: http://t.co/t9qzyXtf #DNC2012
09/05/2012　Reply　Retweet　Favorite

fakejulian Fake Julian Castro
No cops please. She gave it back. RT @thedailybeast: Mayor @JulianCastro's daughter steals the spotlight: http://t.co/jitME8QN #DNC2012
09/05/2012　Reply　Retweet　Favorite

thelepathy thelepathy
#DNC2012-Shootingstar #JulianCastro erinnert fatal an FDP- #Rösler; Töchterchen Carina-V giert nach nem @TiloJung-GIF http://t.co/DRsKI7r0
09/05/2012　Reply　Retweet　Favorite

profealfaro Alma Alfaro
San Antonio Mayor @JulianCastro's daughter steals the spotlight. WATCH: http://t.co/t9qzyXtf #DNC2012
09/05/2012　Reply　Retweet　Favorite

Huffington Post

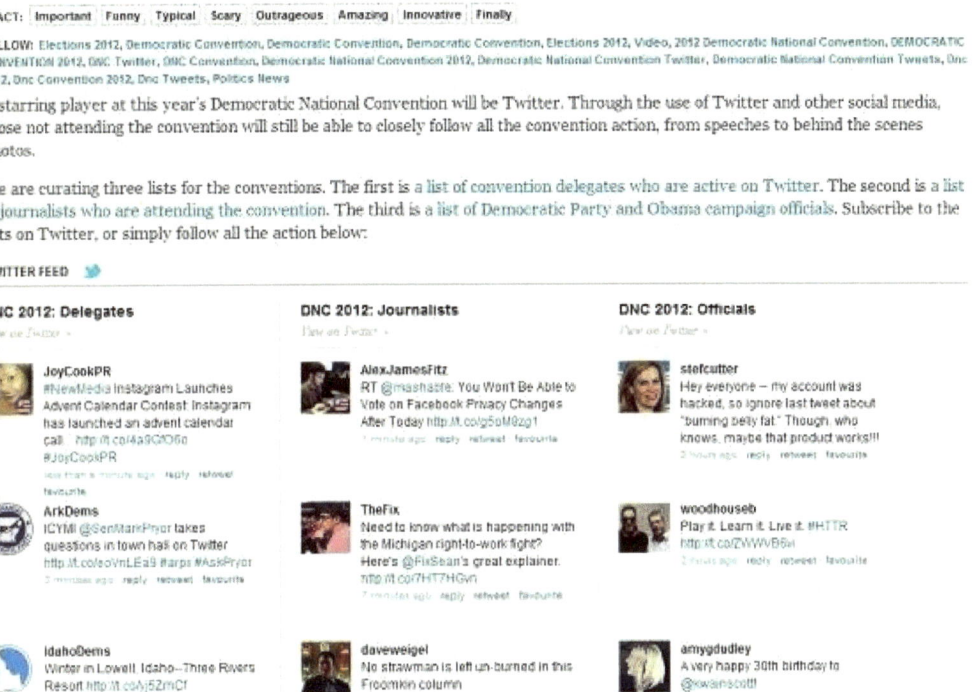

Best Tweets of the 2012 Democratic National Convention

While many speakers were tweeting from backstage, some of the best pictures of the night came the floor of the convention itself. Delegates armed with smartphones brought us all closer to the podium with photos from their points of view. One of the best was @JoyCookPR, a North Carolina delegate, with prime position at the front of the delegates.

> Gov. Tim Kaine of our neighboring state Virginia #DNC2012 twitter.com/JoyCookPR/sta...
>
> — Joy Cook (@JoyCookPR) September 4, 2012

From a position further back, New York delegate @EusicOrtiz was able to show the response of the crowd:

> A sea of FOWARD NOT BACK signs. #dnc2012 twitter.com/eusicortiz/sta...
>
> — Eusic Ortiz (@eusicortiz) September 5, 2012

Keep an eye on the #DNC2012 hashtag page through the rest of the convention this week as people tweet their experiences and reactions. We'll also be tracking more of the big moments on @gov and on the blog.

Posted by Adam Sharp, Head of Government, News, and Social Innovation (@AdamS)

blog.twitter.com

Kicking off #DNC2012

Five million tweets and 600 miles later, the @gov team has landed in Charlotte, ready for another week of speeches, dancing delegates and convention kitsch at #DNC2012. We've launched a new event page, Twitter.com/#DNC2012, where you'll find Tweets about the presidential election straight from the Queen City.

The page will highlight insider views from Obama campaign staffers, featured DNC speakers, Charlotte organizers, delegates and members of the press. Leading up to the opening gavel and tonight's speeches, it will bring those of you who can't be here in Charlotte closer to the planning that goes into this quadrennial rite.

> With Joaquin this morning. Getting ready.
> twitter.com/JulianCastro/s

"While many speakers were tweeting from backstage, some of the best pictures of the night came from the floor of the convention itself. Delegates armed with smartphones brought us all closer to the podium with photos from their points of view. One of the best was @JoyCookPR, a North Carolina delegate, with prime position at the front of the delegates."

 **Joy Cook**
@JoyCook99

 Follow

Gov. Tim Kaine of our neighboring state Virginia #DNC2012
pic.twitter.com/de5FKgs8

4 Sep 12   ← Reply   ↑ Retweet   ★ Favorite

From a position further back, New York delegate @EunicOrtiz was able to show response of the crowd

 **Eunic Ortiz**
@eunicortiz

 Follow

A sea of FOWARD NOT BACK signs. #dnc2012
pic.twitter.com/dluhRV61

In Conclusion

Overall, I don't want to convince you, I want to show you how important it is to carve out your own space on Twitter. This medium has served as a game changer that has ignited movements and jump started careers. Retweets can be endorsements! Taking ownership of your brand by being intentional and strategic on Twitter translates into who I am and what I want you to know. Formulate your Twitter bio today, don't wait!

Follow each of the exercises in this book to make an impact on Twitter. If you are new to Twitter, you want to claim your Twitter handle or Twitter name NOW, because if you wait, it might be already taken. The paradigm has shifted, like it or not.

Whether you are a CEO of a fortune 500 company or the CEO of your own life you should be actively engaging on Twitter. It's a myth that you don't have time to do Twitter, you don't have time NOT to be on Twitter.

We are in the best of times with technology and you want to be where the "magic" is happening.

You could be the next big influencer to be invited to the White House if you, *Watch the Company Your Tweet.*

The Twitter Glossary

The Twitter Glossary includes vocabulary and terminology used to talk about features and aspects of Twitter.

The @ sign is used to call out usernames in Tweets: "Hello @twitter!" People will use your @username to mention you in Tweets, send you a message or link to your profile.

@username

A username is how you're identified on Twitter, and is always preceded immediately by the @ symbol. For instance, Katy Perry is @katyperry.

#

See "hashtag."

Alerts (n.)

Twitter Alerts enable public safety agencies to inform people during emergencies by highlighting critical time-sensitive content with notifications and a unique look.

Bio

Your bio is a short (up to 160 characters) personal description that appears in your profile that serves to characterize your persona on Twitter.

Block

If you block a Twitter user, that account will be unable to follow you or add you to their Twitter lists, and you will not receive a notification if they mention you in a Tweet.

Bug

An internal error in the site code and functionality of Twitter.

Deactivation

If you deactivate your account, it goes into a queue for permanent deletion from Twitter in 30 days. You may reactivate your account within the 30 day grace period.

Direct Message

Use Direct Messages to have private conversations with people you follow who also follow you. Messages have a 140-character limit and can contain text, hashtags, links, photos and video.

Discover

This feature surfaces personalized content tailored to your interests.

Favorite (n.)

Favoriting a Tweet indicates that you liked a specific Tweet. You can find all of your favorite Tweets by clicking on the favorites link on your profile page.

Favorite (v.)

Tap the star icon to favorite a Tweet and the author will see that you liked it.

Follow (v.)

Subscribing to a Twitter account is called "following." To start following, click the Follow button next to the user name or on their profile page to see their Tweets as soon as they post something new. Anyone on Twitter can follow or unfollow anyone else at any time, with the exception of blocked accounts. See "block."

Follow(s) (n.)

A follow is the result of someone following your Twitter account. You can see how many follows (or followers) you have from your Twitter profile.

Follow button

Click the Follow button to follow (or unfollow) anyone on Twitter at any time. When you follow someone, you will see their Tweets in your Home stream.

Follow count

This count reflects how many people you follow and how many follow you; these numbers are found on your Twitter profile.

Follower (n.)

A follower is another Twitter user who has followed you to receive your Tweets in their Home stream.

Geolocation, geotagging

The use of location data in Tweets (a geolocation or geotag) tells those who see your Tweet where you are in real time. You can access the option to "Tweet With Your Location" at the bottom of the "Compose Tweet" box.

Hacking

Gaining unauthorized access to an account via phishing, password guessing, or session stealing. Usually this is followed by unauthorized posts from the account. Hacked accounts are sometimes referred to as "compromised."

Hashflag

A hashflag is a specific series of letters immediately preceded by the # sign which generates an icon on Twitter such as a national flag or another small image.

Hashtag

A hashtag is any word or phrase immediately preceded by the # symbol. When you click on a hashtag, you'll see other Tweets containing the same keyword or topic.

Header photo

Your personal image that you upload, which appears at the top of your profile.

Home

Home is your real-time stream of Tweets from those you follow.

Impersonation

Online impersonation (pretending to be someone you're not) that is intended to deceive is prohibited by Twitter.

List (n.)

From your own account, you can create a group list of other Twitter users by topic or interest (e.g., a list of friends, coworkers, celebrities, athletes). Twitter lists also contain a timeline of Tweets from the specific users that were added to the list, offering you a way to follow individual accounts as a group on Twitter.

Mention (v., n.)

Mentioning other users in your Tweet by including the @ sign followed directly by their username is called a "mention." Also refers to Tweets in which your @username was included.

Mobile web

Twitter's website tailored to fit your mobile device.

Notifications tab, notifications

The Notifications timeline displays your interactions with other Twitter users, like mentions, favorites, Retweets and who has recently followed you.

Parody

You can create parody accounts on Twitter to spoof or make fun of something in jest, as well as commentary and fan accounts. These accounts must disclose that they are parody, fan or commentary accounts in order to comply with strict policy against impersonation.

Phishing

Tricking a user to give up their username and password. This can happen by sending the user to fake sign-in page, a page promising to get you more followers, or just simply asking for the username and password via a DM or email.

Pinned Tweets

You can pin a Tweet to the top of your profile page to keep something important to you above the flow of time-ordered Tweets.

Profile

Your profile displays information you choose to share publicly, as well as all of the Tweets you've posted. Your profile along with your @username identify you on Twitter.

Profile photo

Your personal image found under the Me icon. It's also the picture that appears next to each of your Tweets.

Promoted Accounts

Promoted Accounts present suggested accounts you might want to follow as promoted by advertisers. These appear in your Home timeline, and via Who to Follow, search results and elsewhere on the platform.

Promoted Trends

Promoted Trends display time-, context-, and event-sensitive trends promoted by advertisers. These appear at the top of the Trending Topics list on Twitter and elsewhere on the platform, and are clearly marked as "Promoted."

Promoted Tweets

Promoted Tweets are Tweets that are paid for by advertisers. These appear in your Home timeline, at the top of search results on Twitter and elsewhere on the platform, and are clearly marked as "Promoted."

Protected/private accounts

Twitter accounts are public by default. Choosing to protect your account means that your Tweets will only be seen by approved followers and will not appear in search.

Reply

A response to another user's Tweet that begins with the @username of the person you're replying to is known as a reply. Reply by clicking the "reply" button next to the Tweet you'd like to respond to.

Reactivation

You may reactivate a deactivated account within 30 days of the deactivation date. After 30 days, deactivated accounts are permanently deleted.

Retweet (n.), RT

A Tweet that you forward to your followers is known as a Retweet. Often used to pass along news or other valuable discoveries on Twitter, Retweets always retain original attribution.

Retweet (v.)

The act of sharing another user's Tweet to all of your followers by clicking on the Retweet button.

SMS

Short Message Service (SMS) is most commonly known as text messaging.

Short code

A five-digit phone number used to send and receive Tweets via text message.

Spam

Refers to a variety of prohibited behaviors that violate Twitter rules. Spam can be generally described as unsolicited, repeated actions that negatively impact other users.

Suspended

Suspended accounts have been prohibited from using Twitter, generally for breaking Twitter Terms of Service.

Text commands

When using Twitter via SMS, these commands allow you to access most Twitter features with simple text keywords.

Timeline

A timeline is a real-time stream of Tweets. Your Home stream, for instance, is where you see all the Tweets shared by your friends and other people you follow.

Timestamp

The date and time a Tweet was posted to Twitter. A Tweet's timestamp can be found in grey text in the detail view of any Tweet.

Top Tweets

Tweets determined by a Twitter algorithm to be the most popular or resonant on Twitter at any given time.

Trends

A Trend is a topic or hashtag determined algorithmically to be one of the most popular on Twitter at that moment. You can choose to tailor Trends based on your location and who you follow.

Tweet (n.)

A Tweet may contain photos, videos, links and up to 140 characters of text.

Tweet (v.)

The act of sending a Tweet. Tweets get shown in Twitter timelines or are embedded in websites and blogs.

Tweet button

Anyone can add a Tweet button to their website. Clicking this button lets Twitter users post a Tweet with a link to that site.

Twitter

An information network made up of 140-character messages (including photos, videos and links) from all over the world.

Unfollow (v.)

See "follow" (verb).

URL, URLs

A URL (Uniform Resource Locator) is a web address that points to a unique page on the internet.

Verification

A process whereby a Twitter account receives a blue check icon to indicate that the creator of these Tweets is a legitimate source. Verified users include public figures and those who may have experienced identity confusion on Twitter.

Glossary provided by Twitter

Acknowledgements

First, I want to give glory to my Lord and Savior, Jesus Christ! It is only divine that I have been able to write this book and have such rich experiences using a medium like Twitter.

A VERY special THANK you to my mother, Veda Patrick Cook, who is literally the wind beneath my wings. Not only did my mother give great moral and editing support on this book project. My mother accompanied me to the White House for the TweetUp. As a scientist, my mother challenged me to write this book in a way that it would take the reader on a personal journey of inquisitive exploration.

My babygirl, my daughter, Kayla Cook, I thank you for lending your mommy to this project while you are focusing on your first year of university studies. I am so very proud of you!

My Dad, David Lee Cook the III, the most awesome business man I know. Your business advice trumps Harvard Business School's and I am so thankful I have your advice on speed dial and for free.

To my siblings, Alta Lenee' Braxton and David Lee Cook, IV, their spouses, Mike Braxton and Tiera Cook, respectively, my beautiful nieces and nephew, Bailey, Lucy, and Quint: I love you and thank you for unconditional support and love.

Special acknowledgement goes to my ancestors that have gone home to glory. Their guiding light made sure this project was completed. My angels: Great grandma Mudee (Mary Greene) & Great grandaddy Ben, Grandaddy David Cook, Jr. and Nana, Great grandma Doris Burns, Uncle Bobby, and Uncle Ronald (who passed away on my mother's birthday during the writing of this project).

My mother's and father's siblings: Mother: Uncle Ted, Aunt Peggy,

Aunt Jean, Uncle Ray, Uncle Tony, Uncle Clyde, and Uncle Marcus. Father: Aunt Debra, Aunt Pam, Aunt Margarite, Uncle Larry, Uncle James, Uncle Wesley, and Uncle Reggie. SUPER shout out to Uncle Reggie for his amazing support by coming to the grand opening of my first international office and for purchasing 8 presale books!

To my mentor and friend, Patricia Fairfield-Artman, thank you for lending your expertise to this project and to my life. You taught me PR, strategic communication, and ethics over a decade ago and changed my life in more ways than one. I appreciate you and I am proud to call you, friend.

Thank you, Mary Cantando and the entire Woman's Advantage ® Forum for requiring more of me as a business owner and for teaching me how to "work on my business, not in my business." Special Shout out to Katie Giles for being the first person to suggest I take my rich experience with Twitter and write a book.

There are some friends that unconditionally give you advice. Special thank you to Tracey Simpson my hair stylist (who keeps my camera ready at all times), my sister, and my buddy.

Thank you to William Lee, a publishing GENIUS, you are just getting started!

I would like to thank Rev. Odell Cleveland. Thank you for believing that Twitter is a tool, not a toy and that Twitter will impact your bottom line.

Very special thanks goes out to all of my past and present Joy Cook Public Relations Group Clients, you are the reason I do what I do.

Last but not least, sincere gratitude goes out to President Barack

Obama, First Lady Michelle Obama, and the entire White House Social Staff for the gracious invite and for providing a transparent White House and supporting innovation.

About the Author

Joy Cook is a communications and digital engagement consultant specializing in public relations, publicity, and the art of strategic communication. Her public relations background sets her apart as an outstanding social media strategist and small business coach. She is also an effective and informative speaker.

She has been a lead strategist and manager of key public relations campaigns including the White House acclaimed, Healthcare Faith Community Summit.

As Director of Strategic Communications at Welfare Reform Liaison Project, Inc., Cook was instrumental in developing the organization's collaborative approach to communications and developed its social media strategy. Joy is an experienced professional in making and fostering relationships through digital engagement. This has placed her among top professionals in managing the online community. Joy is affectionately, titled "Ms. Twitter" by the front page of a popular publication and she accepted a special invite to participate in the Arrival Ceremony of British Prime Minister, David Cameron, at a White House Tweetup.

She is a member of the Public Relations Society of America and former Vice President of Public Relations for the Tarheel Chapter. Among her accomplishments are awards for volunteerism. Joy was honored as a Triad Business Journal's 40 Leaders under Forty award recipient.

She chaired the Education Committee for the City of Greensboro, Commission on the Status of Women and represented the 12th Congressional District as Delegate for the Democratic National Convention. Joy is a graduate and current faculty member of the Institute of Political Leadership.

In addition to her accomplishments professionally, Joy is a global volunteer, who is a member of numerous nonprofit boards including, the University of North Carolina at Greensboro, Alumni Association and Guilford College Board of Visitors.

Bibliography

Taking Our Country Back: The Crafting of Networked Politics from Howard Dean to Barack Obama, Oxford University Press, July, 2012.

Kreiss, Daniel. "Acting in the Public Sphere: The 2008 Obama Campaign's Strategic Use of New Media to Shape Narratives of the Presidential Race," Research in Social Movements, Conflict, and Change, 33, 2012.

Jennifer Golbeck, and Derek Hansen. (2011). Computing political preference among twitter followers. Proceedings of CHI 2011. ACM.

Aditi Gupta, and Ponnurangam Kumaraguru. (2012). Credibility Ranking of Tweets during High Impact Events. Workshop on Privacy and Security in Online Social Media Co-located with WWW 2012.